HO...

A detailed descriptive guidebook

on how to build remote controlled

cars aka rc cars for beginners

BRANDON JONES

Table of Contents

CHAPTER ONE

INTRODUCTION

Have you ever felt the rush of driving a little racing machine? The rush coursing through your veins as you negotiate dizzying twists and turns? Welcome to the thrilling world of RC vehicles, where the thrill of the race captivates both young and old.

Consider the perfume of burning rubber, the engine sounds, and the excitement in the air as racers gather around the track. In this cosmos, size doesn't matter; it's the force within that counts. And RC cars, with their tiny frames and strong engines, offer both an exciting and awe-inspiring experience.

I remember seeing my first RC car race. The intensity and excitement in the air was palpable. I couldn't help but be drawn into this intriguing world as I watched the drivers expertly maneuver their automobiles around the circuit, their eyes fixed on the road ahead. It took me a while to realize that RC cars were more than just toys; they represented passion, skill, and pure adrenaline.

The ability of RC cars to captivate people of all ages contributes to their global appeal. The appeal of these miniature racing machines is obvious, whether you're a child enthralled by their remarkable speed and power or an adult reliving childhood happiness. It's inherently fascinating to have a remote control in your hands and drive a vehicle to race, leap, and overcome various terrains.

But the excitement doesn't stop there. Customization and customisation options for RC cars are virtually unlimited. From choosing the ideal body shell to fine-tuning the suspension and drive-train, every aspect of an RC car may be personalized to reflect your personal style and likes. It's a journey of self-expression in which you transform a simple kit into a work of art reflecting your hobbies and personality.

There are various disciplines in the world of RC cars, each with its own set of challenges and rewards. On-road racing delivers an adrenaline rush, with precision and speed working in tandem. Drivers push themselves to the limit around every turn, their sleek, aerodynamic bodies slicing through the air. Then there's the wild realm of off-road racing, where nature becomes your playground. The adrenaline rush of overcoming leaps, sliding through muck, and battling the elements creates a unique experience.

Drift racing is a kind of artistic expression for those who desire to express themselves. This technique blends control precision with the grace of drifting through curves. It's a man-machine dance where grace and style take center stage.

The sound of screaming tires and the hypnotic beauty of controlled slides combine to create a visually gorgeous and exciting experience.

RC cars, on the other hand, deliver more than just an adrenaline rush. This hobby aids in the development of important skills and personality traits. Patience becomes an ally as you meticulously build the fragile components of your RC car. Attention to detail becomes second nature as you fine-tune every aspect for optimal performance. And when you troubleshoot and overcome problems, your problem-solving abilities increase.

In the world of RC cars, you are never alone. The RC car community is a tight-knit group of enthusiasts that adore these little wonders. Whether you're racing against each other, swapping tips and tricks, or simply admiring each other's creations, there's a sense of camaraderie that binds the community together. As you embark on this exciting journey together, the encouragement and support of your fellow enthusiasts generates an environment of growth and learning.

On a sweltering summer day, I happened upon a group of RC car fans in a local park. The adrenaline and the sight of colorful, high-speed vehicles racing around the track drew me in. As I approached, the air was filled with laughter, excitement, and the distinct hum of motors.

Curiosity got the best of me, and I found myself drawn to a group of racers who were excitedly discussing their latest modifications and exchanging tips. Their energy was intoxicating, and I couldn't help but be captivated by their stories and the gleaming RC cars in front of me.

Jake, a kind racer, sensed my enthusiasm and cordially invited me to participate. He handed me a transmitter and instructed me on how to operate an RC car. When I squeezed the trigger, a wave of adrenaline rushed through my veins. My heart was racing alongside the car as it accelerated onward. I couldn't contain my excitement and immediately became immersed in the exhilarating world of RC vehicle racing.

What struck me the most was the racers' fraternity and sportsmanship. Despite the competitive aspect of the sport, there was ongoing support for one another's triumphs and a real readiness to help those in need. The atmosphere was electric, and the racers' relationships established a community that seemed like a family.

Aside from the pure thrill of racing, I discovered that RC cars offered a unique opportunity for personal development. Building and tweaking my own remote-control car taught me patience, attention to detail, and problem-solving skills. It was a journey that required determination and a desire for learning as I delved into the complexity of chassis design, suspension configurations, and electronic combinations.

RC cars not only sparked my interest in engineering and mechanics, but they also instilled in me the importance of teamwork and collaboration. Numerous hours were spent with other enthusiasts exchanging ideas, troubleshooting technical issues, and exchanging performance-enhancing tips. In this society, knowledge was openly exchanged, and the common objective of greatness was evident.

But the greatest impact of my involvement with RC cars was the joy it brought into my life. It became a break from my normal routine, a chance to unwind and immerse myself in an adrenaline-fueled reality. The thrill of pushing my RC car to its limits on the racetrack, the laughter shared with fellow racers, and the sense of accomplishment that comes with each successful build—all of these events have sewn together a tapestry of memories that I will treasure for the rest of my life.

My first encounter with remote-controlled cars was a life-changing experience that brought me to a world of adventure, fellowship, and personal growth. It started a fire inside me that continues to burn brightly to this day. That fateful day at the park set me on a path of exhilarating racing, lasting friendships, and a profound admiration for the power of RC cars.

CHAPTER TWO

IMPORTANCE OF UNDERSTANDING THE FUNDAMENTALS BEFORE DIVING INTO THE BUILD PROCESS

Before beginning the construction process, anyone interested in building an RC car must first comprehend the concepts. It lays the framework for a rewarding and successful building experience, ensuring that you have the knowledge and skills to confront the myriad components and problems that await you. Here are some of the most significant reasons for understanding the fundamentals:

Developing a Solid Knowledge Base: The principles of RC car design, mechanics, and electronics are covered. By familiarizing yourself with these principles, you will gain a greater understanding of how each component performs and interacts with others. This information will allow you to make informed decisions during the construction process, ensuring that you choose the correct parts, make appropriate adjustments, and troubleshoot any problems that may arise.

Ensure Compatibility: RC cars are made up of several components that must work together. Understanding the concepts enables you to locate compatible parts and properly integrate them into your project. From picking the suitable motor and battery to selecting the right transmission system and suspension configuration, a thorough understanding of the fundamentals will prevent compatibility issues and save you time, money, and frustration.

Safety Considerations: When building an RC car, electrical components, batteries, and mechanical elements must be used. It is vital to understand the safety concerns associated with handling these components. Knowing how to properly wire the electronics, maintain batteries, and adhere to safety regulations helps lessen the likelihood of mishaps and ensure a safe building experience.

Efficient Problem-Solving: Building an RC car is a fluid process full of surprises. Understanding the concepts equips you with problem-solving abilities and the ability to effectively resolve difficulties. Whether you're diagnosing electrical difficulties, dealing with mechanical issues, or fine-tuning the performance of your RC car, a solid foundation of knowledge will enable you to recognize and address issues quickly.

Customization and Personalization: One of the most pleasant features of building an RC car is the ability to customize and personalize it. Understanding the fundamentals allows you to make educated selections during the customizing process. From selecting the proper body shell and paint scheme to modifying suspension settings and selecting tires, a good understanding of the fundamentals guarantees that your customizations improve both the aesthetics and performance of your RC car.

Building Confidence: Building an RC car can be a difficult task, especially for beginners. Understanding the fundamentals instills confidence in you since you understand the construction process and the components involved. This assurance helps you to approach the building with enthusiasm and a sense of purpose, knowing that you have the information required to build a high-quality RC car.

Spending time studying the fundamentals before diving into

the building process will ensure a successful and enjoyable experience. It serves as a solid foundation for your RC vehicle-building experience, allowing you to make informed decisions, overcome challenges, and design a customized RC car that reflects your enthusiasm and originality.

BRIEF HISTORY AND EVOLUTION OF RC CARS

RC cars have a unique history dating back to the mid-twentieth century, which includes a spectacular journey of technological advancements and growing popularity. Let's take a short look at some of the major advancements and landmarks that have shaped the world of RC cars:

The First Steps: RC cars were invented in the 1940s and 1950s by enthusiasts and engineers who experimented with remote-controlled vehicles. Early models were often rough and rudimentary, using antiquated radio systems and control procedures.

Commercialization: The first RC cars were sold commercially in the

1960s. Companies such as Mardave and Associated Electrics created small-scale models powered by electric motors. These early RC cars enthralled devotees and laid the framework for the hobby's future growth.

Transition to Nitro-Powered Cars: RC vehicle manufacturers initially launched Nitro-powered vehicles in the 1970s. In terms of speed and performance, nitro engines, which run on a mixture of nitromethane, methanol, and oil, surpassed electric counterparts. The introduction of nitro-powered cars expanded the possibilities of RC car racing and attracted a broader audience.

Technology Advancements: The 1980s were a period of enormous technological advancement in the RC car industry. Manufacturers used proportional radio control systems, allowing for more precise and responsive vehicle control. Improved battery technology and electronic speed controllers substantially improved the performance and runtime of electric RC cars.

Off-Road Revolution: In the 1990s, there was a surge in off-road RC car racing. Off-road automobiles with solid designs and powerful suspension systems were created by manufacturers such as Team Losi and Team Associated. This shift in emphasis from primarily on-road racing to off-road racing presented new opportunities and problems for RC vehicle enthusiasts.

The Digital Transformation Around the turn of the century, there was a digital revolution in RC car technology. Digital proportional radio control systems, which provide even greater control accuracy, became the industry standard. Brushless motors and lithium-polymer (LiPo) batteries have emerged as game changers, enabling quicker speeds, higher power efficiency, and longer runtimes.

Realistic Scale: In recent years, there has been an increasing tendency for scale realism in RC automobiles. Models that are exceptionally faithful in appearance and performance have begun to be produced by manufacturers. This includes accurate body shells, working lights, and detailed interior and engine detailing, which all add to a more immersive experience for enthusiasts.

Integration of Robotics and Artificial Intelligence: Advances in robotics and artificial intelligence have begun to influence the world of RC autos. Some models now have features like as autonomous driving, GPS navigation, and obstacle detection and avoidance systems. This combination of RC cars and cutting-edge technology gives up exciting possibilities for the hobby's future.

RC cars have become a worldwide sensation, attracting fans of all ages and skill levels. The pastime is growing in popularity as technology, materials, and design improve. From backyard races to official events, RC car racing has evolved into a thrilling and competitive sport that brings people together, creating a vibrant community of fans who share a passion for the world of RC cars.

DIFFERENT TYPES OF RC CARS AND THEIR UNIQUE CHARACTERISTICS

There are various types of RC cars, each designed for a certain function and environment. Let's have a look at some of the most common types of RC cars and their distinguishing characteristics:

Vehicles Used on the Road: On-road RC cars are designed for high-speed racing on smooth surfaces such as asphalt or concrete. For better stability and lower drag, they have low-profile tires, aerodynamic body shells, and lower ground clearance. On-road cars thrive in terms of speed, cornering, and overall performance on level and even ground.

Off-Road Cars: These RC vehicles are built to handle rough and uneven terrains including dirt, gravel, grass, and off-road tracks.

They have more ground clearance, larger and knobbly tires, powerful suspension systems, and durable chassis that can withstand shocks and bumps. Off-road vehicles are known for their adaptability and ability to manage a wide range of outdoor conditions, which makes them ideal for dangerous racing and bashing.

Drift Vehicles: RC cars designed exclusively for controlled drifting. Slick or drift-specific tires, a lightweight chassis, and a rear-wheel-drive (RWD) configuration allow for controlled slides and drift motions. Drift cars emphasize sideways sliding and precise control over overall speed, emulating the exciting nature of actual drift racing.

Rock Crawlers: Remote-controlled rock crawlers are meant to navigate challenging terrains such as rocks, steep inclines, and obstructions. High torque engines, articulated suspension systems, massive and grippy tires, and cutting-edge four-wheel-drive (4WD) configurations are all standard. Rock crawlers emphasize slow and controlled motions, precise handling, and maximum traction to navigate risky off-road paths.

Monster trucks are characterised by their enormous size, large wheels, and outstanding off-road performance. They are designed to cross difficult terrain, perform high leaps, and perform amazing acrobatics. Monster trucks have powerful suspension systems, massive tires, and sturdy chassis to withstand the punishment of extreme jumps and landings.

Short Course Trucks are miniature versions of full-size off-road racing trucks. They are built to race on closed, off-road tracks with jumps, banked curves, and a variety of hazards. Short course trucks are built to resist the demands of high-speed racing and aggressive driving, with massive all-terrain tires and long-lasting suspension systems.

Buggies: RC buggies combine the qualities of on-road and off-road vehicles to provide versatility and agility. They are lightweight and aerodynamic, with all-terrain tires and adjustable suspension systems. Buggies are well-suited for both on-road racing and off-road circuits due to their combination of speed, maneuverability, and off-road expertise.

Some categories may overlap, and particular RC cars are designed to perform well in a variety of settings. Furthermore, technology advances and customization options have resulted in hybrid models that may be tailored to different racing preferences and terrains.

The type of RC car you choose is decided by your intended use, racing preferences, and the environment in which you expect to drive. There is an RC car type that will suit your racing style and deliver an entertaining experience, whether you enjoy high-speed on-road racing, tackling off-road trails, doing precise drift maneuvers, or conquering tough rock formations.

CHAPTER THREE

KEY COMPONENTS OF AN RC CAR

A radio-controlled car is comprised of multiple critical components that operate in tandem to ensure its performance, handling, and operation. Let's have a look at the major components of an RC car:

Chassis: The chassis serves as the foundation of the RC car, providing structural support and housing the various components. Aluminum, carbon fiber, and composite polymers are among of the lightweight yet strong elements employed in its construction. The chassis design may differ depending on the type of RC car, with varied layouts for on-road, off-road, and specialty vehicles.

Suspension System: The suspension system is essential for maintaining traction, absorbing shocks, and providing stability under various driving conditions. It is composed of shocks, springs, and linkages that let the wheels to move independently, allowing for best ground contact. The suspension system is adjustable, allowing you to fine-tune the vehicle's handling characteristics.

The drivetrain transfers power from the motor to the wheels, allowing the RC car to move. The motor, transmission, differential, and drive shafts are all part of it. Front-wheel drive (FWD), rear-wheel drive (RWD), and four-wheel drive (4WD) are all options for the drivetrain. The type of RC car and its intended application dictate the drivetrain.

Electronics: An RC car's electronics control the vehicle's movement, steering, and power distribution. They include a radio transmitter and receiver, an electronic speed controller (ESC), steering servo motors, and any other features such as sound systems or lighting. These electronics work together to provide accurate control and reaction to the driver's inputs.

The motor is the heart of an RC car, providing mechanical energy for propulsion. For jobs like rock crawling or high-speed racing, RC cars can use a range of motors, including brushed, brushless, and speciality motors. The power and performance of the motor have a direct impact on the speed and acceleration of the RC car.

The battery provides electricity to the motor as well as other electronic components. In RC cars, nickel-metal hydride (NiMH) and lithium-polymer (LiPo) batteries are often utilized. The capacity and voltage of the battery determine the runtime and power output of the RC car. It is vital to select a battery that is compatible with the motor and ESC system.

Tires and wheels: The wheels and tires determine traction, grip, and handling. Tire tread patterns and compound compositions vary, and RC car wheels can be made of various materials such as plastic or metal. Depending on the type of RC car and the surface it will be driven on, several tire types and sizes are used to optimise performance.

Body Shell: The body shell is the outside covering of the RC car, providing both beauty and protection for the interior components. Body shells are frequently made of lightweight polycarbonate or similar materials that may be customized with paint schemes and decals. The body shell also aids in aerodynamics and can be designed to seem like a real car.

The steering system directs the movement of the remote control car. It is typically composed of a servo motor, linkages, and a steering system that converts radio transmitter data into precise steering movements. The steering mechanism's quickness and accuracy are crucial for maintaining control and maneuverability.

The portable devices used by the RC car driver to relay commands to the car are the transmitter and receiver. It sends signals wirelessly to the receiver, which is attached to the RC car. The transmitter and receiver work together to create a dependable and responsive communication link, allowing the driver to control the vehicle's speed, direction, and other functions.

Body Clips and Mounts: These components connect the body shell to the chassis. Body mounts hold the body shell in place, while clips or pins keep it in place. They make removing and replacing the body shell straightforward, which is beneficial for maintenance, customizing, or swapping between different body designs.

Bearings are tiny precision-engineered components that help to reduce friction between rotating elements. They are extensively used in drivetrain and suspension systems to produce smooth and efficient movement. High-quality bearings help to reduce power loss while also boosting overall performance.

Shocks: Shocks, also known as dampers, are suspension system components that absorb impacts and maintain stability. They employ oil or gas-filled cylinders to decrease suspension movement, hence enhancing handling and lowering chassis vibrations.

Gearing is the gear ratio that exists between the motor and the wheels. It determines the speed and torque characteristics of the RC car. To modify the gearing, the pinion gear (linked to the engine) and spur gear (attached to the drivetrain) can be changed. Proper gearing selection is crucial for optimizing performance and staying within the motor's specified parameters.

Extras available as options include: A multitude of different accessories can improve the operation and performance of an RC car. Additional lighting, sound systems, telemetry modules for monitoring battery voltage and speed, suspension upgrades, and specialty components for specific applications like as racing or rock crawling may be provided. These attachments provide modification options, allowing enthusiasts to tailor their RC cars to their own preferences and requirements.

Remember that the exact components and their combinations will vary depending on the type, brand, and model of RC car. Follow the manufacturer's instructions and suggestions for your individual RC car to ensure proper knowledge and utilization of the components.

ESSENTIAL TOOLS AND EQUIPMENT FOR BUILDING AND MAINTAINING RC CARS

It is vital to have the proper tools and equipment for building and maintaining RC cars in order to have a smooth and successful experience. Here are some of the tools and equipment required:

Screwdrivers: A set of screwdrivers of various sizes and types (such as Phillips and flathead) will be necessary for assembling and removing various pieces of the RC car.

Allen wrenches, also known as hex keys, are used to tighten and loosen hex screws, which are commonly found in RC cars. A set of Allen wrenches in various sizes will ensure that you have the right tools for the job.

Nut drivers are used to tighten and loosen nuts, particularly those found on axles and engine mounts. It will be easier to maintain your RC car if you have a set of nut drivers that match the sizes of the nuts used.

Pliers are versatile tools that can be used to grab and hold small parts, bend wires, and remove and insert body clips.

For cutting and trimming materials like body shells or decals, a hobby knife with sharp and replaceable blades is excellent. It's also useful for removing extra flashing from plastic parts.

Needle nose pliers have long, narrow jaws that allow them to reach and hold small or difficult-to-reach items. They are extremely useful for working with cables, connections, and other fragile components.

Wire cutters are required to cut and trim wires to the proper lengths. They ensure clean and exact cuts, which is crucial for maintaining the electrical connections on the RC car.

Soldering Iron and Solder: A soldering iron and solder are required if you wish to undertake more difficult alterations or repairs that require soldering electronic components. This allows you to create safe electrical connections or repair damaged cables or connectors.

Battery Charger: A dependable battery charger is required for charging the batteries in your RC car. Depending on the type of batteries you use (such as NiMH or LiPo), make sure you have a compatible charger with the necessary charging modes and safety features.

Setup tools are specialized tools used to fine-tune and alter many aspects of your RC car, such as ride height, camber, toe-in/out, and suspension settings. These tools include ride height gauges, camber gauges, droop gauges, and shock manufacturing tools.

Cleaning Supplies: In order for your RC car to function and last, it must be kept clean. Cleaning supplies including brushes, compressed air canisters, and cleaning solutions will help you remove dirt, dust, and debris from your car's components.

Spare Parts and Accessories: It's always a good idea to keep a supply of spare parts and accessories on hand, such as extra screws, gears, bearings, suspension arms, or body clips. This allows you to quickly replace worn or broken parts for maintenance or repairs.

Keep in mind that the tools and equipment you'll need may vary depending on the type of RC car you have and the jobs you intend to do. Always follow the manufacturer's recommendations and instructions for any special tools or equipment required for your specific RC car model.

RESEARCHING AND SELECTING THE RIGHT RC CAR KIT OR CHASSIS

Researching and selecting the right RC vehicle kit or chassis is a vital step in building your own RC car. Here are some pointers to get you started:

Determine your goals and preferences: Consider the desired use and goals of the RC car. Do you like quick racing, off-road adventures, or precision drifting? Understanding your tastes will allow you to narrow down your options and choose a kit or chassis that will provide you the necessary experience.

Look into several brands and models: Investigate a variety of RC car manufacturers and models to get a sense of what's available. Read reviews, watch videos, and visit RC vehicle forums to gain insights and comments from experienced hobbyists. This inquiry will provide you a better understanding of the quality, performance, and reputation of several options.

Consider the following sorts of RC cars: Choose whether you want to build an on-road car, an off-road buggy, a drift car, a rock crawler, or another type of specialized RC car. Each type has distinct traits, components, and performance characteristics. Select a kit or chassis tailored for the type of RC car you want to build.

Consider Your Experience and Skill Level: Consider your experience and skill level in the construction and assembly of RC vehicles. Some kits or chassis may be more suitable for beginners, with simple assembly and clear instructions, while others may require more advanced technical knowledge and skills. Choose a kit that matches to your skill level to ensure a successful build.

Quality and durability: Take note of the quality and lifespan of the kit or chassis. Look for materials with a strong and durable reputation, such as high-grade plastics or carbon fiber components. Read user reviews to get a sense of the kit's overall quality and longevity.

There are spare parts and technical help available: Check the kit or chassis's spare parts and customer service availability. It's essential to keep spare parts on hand in case you need to repair or alter your RC car in the future. Consider whether there is technical support or online groups where you can get help.

Budget: Set a budget for your RC car project, including the cost of the kit or chassis, as well as any additional components or electronics required to complete the build. Remember to factor in the cost of any additional batteries, chargers, equipment, or accessories that may be required.

Compatibility and Customization: If you wish to personalize or modify your RC car in the future, consider the compatibility of the kit or chassis with aftermarket components and upgrades. Having a wide range of compatible components accessible will provide you more customization and performance-enhancing options.

Examine the Package Contents: Examine the kit's or chassis package's contents to ensure that it contains all of the necessary components. Look for complete kits that include all of the necessary components such as the chassis, suspension, drivetrain, and body shell.

Seek Advice and Suggestions: Don't be scared to seek guidance from experienced RC vehicle enthusiasts or hobby shop specialists. They can provide valuable insights and recommendations based on their knowledge and experience.

If you thoroughly research and select the perfect RC vehicle kit or chassis, you'll lay the groundwork for a fun construction experience and a high-performance RC car that meets your expectations.

CHAPTER FOUR

UNDERSTANDING DIFFERENT SCALES AND THEIR IMPLICATIONS

Understanding the different scales of RC cars is crucial for selecting the best size and understanding the implications for the vehicle's performance and handling. The following is a list of the most frequent RC car scales and their implications:

1/10 Scale: This is one of the most widely used RC car scales. In this scale, the RC car is around one-tenth the size of its real-life counterpart. 1/10 scale RC cars offer an excellent balance of size, performance, and cost. They are versatile and widely available, providing an excellent blend of speed and control for a wide range of racing and off-road applications.

Scale: 1/8 scale RC automobiles are larger than 1/10 scale models, around one-eighth the size of real vehicles. These vehicles are well-known for their strength and longevity. 1/8 scale RC cars are commonly used for off-road racing since their larger size allows for better performance on uneven terrain. They frequently have more powerful engines, larger tires, and more suspension travel.

Scale of 1/5: Scale of 1/5 RC automobiles are significantly larger, around one-fifth the size of real cars. These vehicles demand attention and are typically outfitted with powerful gasoline or electric engines. Because of their size, 1/5 scale RC cars are frequently used for on-road racing or large off-road locations. They provide exceptional stability, quick speeds, and long runtimes.

1/18 Scale: 1/18 Scale: 1/18 Scale 1/10 scale RC cars are smaller and lighter than RC automobiles. These cars are ideal for indoor racing, tight tracks, or compact spaces. Because of their small size, they have slower speeds, yet they can still deliver pleasant and competitive racing experiences.

Scales Not Included: Other less common scales are 1/12, 1/14, and 1/16. These scales are typically used for certain RC car categories like as micro racing, rock crawlers, and specialty vehicles. Each scale has its own particular features and functionalities that cater to specific preferences and applications.

Consequences of Scale:

a) Size and transportation: The scale of an RC car influences its size and transportation. Larger scales, such as 1/8 and 1/5, may require more storage and transportation, but smaller sizes, such as 1/18, are more compact and easier to handle.

b) Speed and Performance: Larger scale RC cars generally have higher speeds and more powerful performance. They often have larger engines, better suspension systems, and more stability, resulting in greater acceleration and top speeds.

c) Handling and Maneuvrability: Smaller RC cars, such as 1/18 or 1/12, are more agile and nimble, making them excellent for tight tracks or indoor racing. Larger sizes, such as 1/8 or 1/5, offer better stability and handling on rough terrain or quick courses.

d) Cost: The cost of an RC car is determined on its size. Because of their larger size, more modern components, and higher performance capabilities, larger scale models are often more expensive. Smaller scale models are often more affordable and accessible, making them a good choice for beginners or budget-conscious hobbyists.

Before selecting an RC car, consider your preferences,

intended use, available space, and budget. Understanding the effects of different scales will help you make an informed decision and choose an RC car that matches your needs while also delivering a joyful driving experience.

DECODING TECHNICAL JARGON AND SPECIFICATIONS

Decoding technical jargon and specs in the realm of RC cars can be confusing for newbies. To assist you understand the meanings and implications of popular terms and requirements, below are some definitions:

The type of motor used in an RC car is referred to as the motor type. The two most common varieties are brushed and brushless motors. Brushed motors are simpler, less expensive, and better suited to entry-level models. Brushless motors are more advanced and efficient, providing better performance and longevity.

KV Rating: A brushless motor's rotational speed is determined by its KV rating. It indicates the number of revolutions per minute (RPM) the motor will make per volt of input. Higher KV ratings indicate faster speeds, whilst lower KV levels indicate more torque for better acceleration and climbing.

Battery Type and Voltage: Rechargeable batteries, the most common of which are Nickel Metal Hydride (NiMH) and Lithium Polymer (LiPo), are often used in RC cars. Battery voltage is measured in volts (V) and measures the power output of the battery. Higher voltage batteries offer greater power and speed, but they also demand appropriate circuitry and handling.

ESC (Electronic Speed Controller): The ESC controls speed and acceleration by directing power from the battery to the motor. It also has braking, reverse functionality, and user-configurable settings. ESCs are custom-made to match the motor type and voltage of the RC car.

Suspension Type: The suspension system of an RC car determines its handling, stability, and ability to absorb shocks. Two typical suspension systems are independent suspension, which allows greater control and handling on varying terrains, and solid axle suspension, which provides more stability and durability for off-road or crawling applications.

The radio system is made up of two parts: the transmitter (controller) and the receiver. It allows you to wirelessly control the RC car's motions and functions. To provide consistent and interference-free communication between the transmitter and receiver, radio systems use many frequency bands, such as 2.4GHz.

The gear ratio defines the connection between motor rotation and wheel rotation. Lower gear ratios offer more torque for acceleration and climbing, whilst higher gear ratios allow for faster top speeds. To modify the gear ratio, adjust the pinion gear (linked to the motor) and spur gear (attached to the drivetrain).

Body Type: The body type refers to the style and design of the RC car's external shell. Aerodynamic bodies, for example, are great for high-speed racing, as are scale replica bodies for realistic appearances.

Tread Patterns and Tires: The tires and tread patterns used in an RC car affect its traction, grip, and performance on varied surfaces. Off-road tires with deeper treads have better traction on rough or uneven terrain, but on-road tires with slick or semi-slick patterns have superior grip on level ground.

Scale: The scale refers to the size of the RC automobile in comparison to its real-life counterpart. The most commonly used scales are 1/10, 1/8, and 1/5, which represent fractions of real size. The scale determines overall size, performance characteristics, replacement parts and equipment availability, and so on.

Some RC cars are waterproof or water-resistant, allowing them to be utilized in wet or humid conditions. Waterproofing is especially important for off-road vehicles, which may come into contact with water, dirt, or rain while in use.

Consult the manufacturer's specs and user manuals for specific information about your RC car. Understanding these technical terms and specifications will help you make informed decisions, troubleshoot difficulties, and improve your overall RC car experience.

CHAPTER FIVE

EXPLORING VARIOUS POWER OPTIONS

Electric, nitro, and gas RC vehicle engines are the three fundamental types to consider. Each option has its own set of advantages and disadvantages. Let us investigate these further:

Rechargeable batteries, most often Nickel Metal Hydride (NiMH) or Lithium Polymer (LiPo), power electric RC cars.

Advantages:

Easy to use and maintain: Electric RC cars are frequently simpler to operate and maintain than their nitro or gas counterparts.

Quieter and more sanitary: Electric motors emit no exhaust fumes and produce less noise, making them suitable for use both indoors and outdoors in noise-sensitive areas.

Electric motors deliver immediate torque and acceleration, enabling quick acceleration and responsiveness.

There are several options: Electric RC cars come in a variety of sizes, styles, and performance levels, making them appropriate for beginners, enthusiasts, and specialists alike.

Electric RC cars have lower runtimes than nitro or gas-powered cars. The runtime is determined by the battery capacity, which can range from a few minutes to more than half an hour.

Time it takes to charge the batteries: Charging the batteries can take some time, especially if they are greater in capacity. Spare batteries or a fast charger are necessary for continuing enjoyment.

While there are many different price points for electric RC vehicles, high-performance electric versions might be more expensive than entry-level nitro or gas cars.

Nitro RC cars are propelled by miniature internal combustion engines powered by nitro-methane fuel.

Advantages:

Realistic sound and smell: Nitro engines emit exhaust fumes and have a distinct engine sound, resulting in a more authentic and immersive experience.

Long runtimes: Nitro RC cars can run for a long time on a single tank of gas, allowing for longer play sessions.

Nitro engines allow fans to fine-tune performance, throttle response, and fuel mixture for optimal performance.

Considerations:

Complex operation and maintenance: Nitro RC cars require more technical expertise and maintenance than electric cars. Routine maintenance includes cleaning the engine, tweaking carburetors, and changing glow plugs.

Engine noise and exhaust emissions may restrict usage in some areas or need consideration for noise pollution and environmental legislation.

Nitro gasoline is more difficult to obtain than electric charging options, and it raises the overall operating cost.

Small two-stroke or four-stroke gasoline engines, similar to those found in lawnmowers and chainsaws, power gas RC cars.

Long runtimes: Because gas RC cars have longer runtimes, they can be used for longer periods of time with less frequent recharging.

Power and realistic engine sound: When compared to nitro or electric engines, gas engines produce more power and have more realistic engine sounds.

Gas engines, like nitro engines, have tuning options that allow enthusiasts to adjust performance and enhance power delivery.

Considerations:

Greater complexity and care: When compared to electric versions, gas RC cars necessitate greater technical knowledge and upkeep. Tuning the engine, adjusting the fuel mixture, and maintaining it on a regular basis are all required.

Noise and exhaust emissions: Gas engines, like nitro engines, emit noise and exhaust emissions, which may restrict their usage in some areas or need compliance with noise and environmental requirements.

Fuel cost and availability: While gasoline is more generally available than nitro fuel, proper storage and handling are required. As a result, operating costs may be higher.

PREPARING YOUR WORKSPACE AND ORGANIZING YOUR TOOLS

To have a productive and enjoyable RC vehicle assembly and maintenance experience, it is necessary to arrange your workstation and organize your supplies. Here are some tips to help you organize and effective workspace:

Organization of the Workplace: Begin by removing any clutter or unnecessary objects from your workspace. A neat and spacious workspace will allow you to work comfortably while reducing the possibility of misplacing small pieces or tools.

Ample Lighting: Ensure that your desk is well-lit. Ample lighting allows you to clearly see minute features and components, reducing the likelihood of mistakes during the construction or maintenance process.

Workbench or Table: Build a sturdy workbench or table to use as a dedicated workspace for your RC car tasks. A smooth and solid surface will make it easy to assemble, disassemble, and operate on various components of your RC car.

Storage Containers, Bins, or Drawers: Buy storage containers, bins, or drawers to arrange your tools, spare parts, and accessories. Make your own method by labeling each container for easy identification. Separating small parts, screws, nuts, and bolts into different compartments will save you time and effort while searching for certain items.

Tool Storage: Make a place for your tools. Consider using a tool tray, pegboard, or tool chest to keep your equipment organized and easily accessible. Arrange them in a logical order, such as screwdrivers next to wrenches, and so forth.

Magnetic Tray: A magnetic tray can be used to organize small metal parts such as screws, washers, and clips. Cable Management: Organize your workplace by managing cords and wires. To keep wires from tangling or disrupting your workspace, secure and organize them with cable ties, clips, or cable management sleeves.

Always put safety equipment first. Maintain convenient access to safety items in your workplace, such as goggles, gloves, and dust masks. This will ensure that you are safe when working with chemicals, power tools, or sharp things.

Research Materials: Keep handy reference materials such as RC car manuals, building instructions, and online resources. They will give you important advice and directions.

CHAPTER SIX

TROUBLESHOOTING TIPS DURING THE BUILD OR MAINTENANCE PROCESS

own Comfort: Keep your own comfort in mind when working on your RC car. Use a comfortable chair or stool that allows you to sit at the correct height. While working for lengthy periods of time, consider using a floor mat or cushioning to provide support and reduce pressure on your feet and legs.

By following these tips, you can create an organized and efficient workspace that will enhance your RC car production and maintenance experience. A well-organized workspace not only saves you time and effort, but it also lets you to concentrate on the task at hand and enjoy working on your RC cars.

EFFECTIVELY READING AND INTERPRETING INSTRUCTION MANUALS

Reading and analyzing instruction manuals effectively is essential for understanding the design and operation of your RC car. Here are some tips to help you make the most of your instruction manuals:

Examine the Complete Manual: Before undertaking any assembly or operation, read the whole instruction manual from start to finish. This will provide you a thorough understanding of the process and will assist you in anticipating any barriers or tools that may be required.

Instructions in Steps: Instruction manuals are frequently set out in a step-by-step format. To prevent missing any important facts or procedures, proceed through the stages in the correct order, without skipping any. Take your time with each step and make sure you understand the instructions before proceeding.

Keep an eye out for warnings and safety precautions: Instruction manuals usually offer critical safety information and cautions. Read and comprehend these components thoroughly to ensure your safety and the proper operation of your RC car. Follow any safety precautions outlined in the handbook.

Make use of visual aids: In instruction manuals, diagrams, images, and photographs are routinely used to clarify assembly or operating procedures. Pay close attention to these visual aids since they might provide clarity and support.

Highlight important portions or directions with highlighters or take notes as you read through the booklet. This will allow you to quickly refer to critical information in the future. Making a list of any queries or problems you are experiencing might also help you gain clarification or fix.

Seek Clarification: If a step or instruction is unclear or baffling to you, don't be hesitant to ask for clarification. Consult internet forums, RC car communities, or manufacturer support channels for assistance. It is vital to have a firm understanding before commencing to avoid mistakes or potential issues.

Understand the Terminology: Technical terms specific to the hobby may appear in RC car instruction manuals. Take the time to learn these terms so that you can fully comprehend the instructions. Visit a glossary or online resources to gain a better understanding of an unfamiliar term.

Divide Complex Steps: If a task looks to be complex or overwhelming, break it down into smaller, more manageable jobs. By dividing the procedure down into smaller sub-steps, you may approach it more systematically and reduce the chances of error.

As You Go Testing: Whenever possible, test the functioning of components or full assemblies as you make your way through the guide. This allows you to identify any issues early on and ensure that everything is functioning properly before continue.

Save the manual for future reference: Once the assembly or operation procedure is completed, save the manual for future reference. It can help with RC car maintenance, troubleshooting, and learning about certain qualities.

By following these advice, you will be able to properly read and interpret instruction manuals, ensuring a smooth and successful experience with your RC car. Remember that following the instructions and building a high-quality RC car take time and attention to detail.

ASSEMBLING THE CHASSIS AND INSTALLING KEY COMPONENTS

Assembling the chassis and attaching crucial components is a critical stage in building your RC car. Proper assembly ensures the structural integrity and performance of your vehicle. Here's a step-by-step guide to get you started:

Gather the Required Tools and Components: Before you begin, gather all of the tools and components listed in the instruction booklet. Screwdrivers, wrenches, pliers, and the chassis itself may be included, as well as other components such as the suspension system, drivetrain, and electronics.

Acquaint yourself with the chassis: Take a minute to familiarize acquainted with the chassis's numerous components. Determine the main structure, suspension mounting locations, motor mounting location, battery compartment, and any other significant aspects of your RC car model.

Start by attaching the suspension system to the chassis. Install the shocks, arms, and other suspension components as directed in the handbook. Pay great attention to how each component is oriented and aligned.

Install the Drivetrain: Next, assemble the drivetrain components (gearbox, differential, and drive shafts). Make that the gears are properly meshing and aligned, and that the drive shafts are securely attached to the wheels and gearbox.

Install the Motor: If your RC car is electric, install the motor in the proper spot on the chassis. Check that it is properly aligned with the gear mesh and securely fastened with the necessary screws or clamps.

Set up the Electronics: Place the electronic components, such as the receiver, ESC, servo, and battery, in their respective locations. Follow the instructions in the manual for proper placement and wiring of these components. Keep an eye out for polarity and make sure all connections are tight.

Secure Wiring and Cables: Arrange and secure the wiring and cables so that they do not interfere with or become tangled with moving parts. Use zip ties, cable clips, or routing channels to neatly fasten and route the wires around the chassis.

Check Alignment and fitting: Once all of the components have been installed, thoroughly inspect the chassis to guarantee proper alignment and fitting. Check the suspension arms for smooth movement, the engine for free rotation, and that all components are securely fastened.

Test the functionality of the chassis and crucial components before proceeding with further assembly or adjustments. Examine the suspension for smooth compression and rebound, the drivetrain for proper power transmission, and the electronics for proper response to transmitter commands.

As needed, make the following changes: Make any necessary corrections if any flaws or misalignments are identified during the functionality test. This includes repositioning components, changing gear mesh, and fine-tuning suspension settings. Consult the instruction manual or get guidance from experienced RC hobbyists if necessary.

Photograph and documentation: Consider photographing and documenting your progress during the assembly process. This can come in handy for future reference, troubleshooting, or sharing your construction experience with others.

Remember to follow the assembly instructions in the handbook that came with your RC car, since they may vary depending on the model. For a well-built and dependable RC vehicle chassis, take your time, carefully follow the instructions, and ensure that every component is firmly attached.

MOTOR AND TRANSMISSION MOUNTING

Mounting the motor and transmission is a critical step in the RC car production process. Proper installation ensures that power is efficiently delivered from the motor to the wheels. Here's a step-by-step guide to get you started:

Prepare the engine and transmission: Check to see that you have the motor, transmission, and any necessary mounting brackets or plates for your RC car model.

Determine the Engine Mounting Place: Consult the instruction manual to locate the suitable motor installation area on the chassis of your RC car. The manual will normally offer extensive diagrams or descriptions to assist you.

Align the motor mounting holes in the following manner: Align the mounting holes on the motor with the corresponding holes on the motor mounting zone of the chassis. Examine the motor's position in respect to the drivetrain and gear mesh.

Attach the Motor Mounting Plate or Bracket as follows: If your RC vehicle model has one, place the motor mounting plate or bracket over the motor, aligning the holes with the motor mounting point. Securely fasten the plate or bracket with the provided screws.

modify the Gear Mesh: If your RC car has a gear-driven transmission, you must modify the gear mesh between the motor pinion gear and the transmission spur gear. Consult the instruction manual for specific directions on setting the right gear mesh.

After the motor and transmission have been properly aligned and the gear mesh has been adjusted, use the necessary screws to fasten the motor to the motor mounting site. Check that the motor is firmly attached and that it is not moving excessively.

If your RC car is electric, connect the motor wires to the electronic speed controller (ESC) as recommended. Maintain a solid connection by paying close attention to polarity.

Route the motor cables and any other associated cabling neatly along the chassis, using zip ties or cable clips to secure them. Check that there are no moving parts or components interfering with the wiring.

Examine Clearance and Alignment: Make sure there is enough space between the motor and transmission assembly and the rest of the chassis components. Ensure that there is no interference or binding during operation. Check for misalignments and make any necessary corrections.

Before proceeding with additional assembly or alterations, ensure that the motor functions well. Connect the battery and transmitter, and verify that the motor responds appropriately to throttle inputs. Keep an eye out for any strange noises or vibrations.

Make Any Required modifications: Make any necessary modifications if any issues or concerns arise during the testing phase. This could include fine-tuning the gear mesh, repositioning the motor, or dealing with any performance difficulties. Consult the instruction instructions or get guidance from experienced RC hobbyists if necessary.

Because the mounting technique differs depending on the model, always follow the instructions in your RC car's manual. To ensure a safe and dependable motor and transmission assembly, take your time, carefully follow the recommendations, and double-check all connections and alignments.

INSTALLING THE SUSPENSION SYSTEM

Installing the suspension system is a vital step in building your RC car. The suspension system is essential for providing stability, handling, and control on a range of terrains. Here's a step-by-step guide to get you started:

Determine Suspension Parts: Gather all of the suspension parts listed in the instruction manual. Shock absorbers, suspension arms, hinge pins, ball ends, and other components may be included.

Identify the Suspension Design: Consider the suspension design of your RC car for a bit. Determine the suspension systems in the front and back, the kind of suspension (e.g., independent or solid axle), and any model-specific features.

Suspension arms must be attached as follows: Begin by attaching the suspension arms to the appropriate mounting points on the chassis. The front and rear arms of your RC car may be separate. Use the provided screws or hinge pins to fasten the arms.

Install the shock absorbers on the suspension arms and shock towers. Consult the instruction manual for the precise orientation and mounting positions. To secure the shock absorbers, use the appropriate screws or ball ends.

Suspension Settings: Some RC cars include adjustable suspension settings, such as ride height, damping, and spring tension. Consult the owner's manual to understand how to change these settings and fine-tune the suspension to your liking or the terrain.

Check Suspension Alignment: Once the suspension components have been installed, check sure that all suspension arms and shocks are properly aligned. Check that the suspension arms may move freely and without interference from other components.

Suspension Movement: Compress and release each suspension arm to ensure that the suspension is working properly. Examine the suspension for smooth, responsive movement and that it rebounds without excessive bouncing or sagging.

Fine-Tune Suspension Performance: Make slight adjustments to the suspension settings to achieve the desired performance. Experiment with varied spring tensions and shock placements to improve your RC car's handling.

Wires and cables that are secure: While installing the suspension system, make sure that any wires or cables are carefully routed and fastened. To avoid interference with the suspension components, utilize zip ties, cable clips, or routing channels to maintain the arrangement neat and tidy.

Conduct a Functionality Test: Test the suspension system's functionality before proceeding with any assembly or alterations.

Rock or drive the RC car gently to watch how it reacts to various surfaces and barriers. Make any necessary modifications or fine-tuning based on your observations.

Repeat the installation procedure for the other suspension components if your RC car has separate front and rear suspension systems.

Because suspension installation procedures vary by model, always follow the specific directions provided in your RC car's manual. Take your time, carefully follow the instructions, and ensure that all suspension components are properly installed for the maximum performance, stability, and control of your RC car.

WHEELS, TIRES, AND AXLES ATTACHMENT

Attaching your RC car's wheels, tires, and axles is an important step that affects its performance and handling. Here's a step-by-step guide to get you started:

Collect the Materials: Collect all of the wheels, tires, axles, wheel nuts or hex nuts, and other components required for your specific RC car model. Check that you have the right size and kind of wheels and tires for the job.

Create the Axles: Keep your RC car's separate axles clean and free of dirt and debris. Apply a small amount of grease or lubricant to the axle shafts to minimize friction and aid in smooth rotation.

Slide the wheels onto the axles, making sure they are secure against any wheel hubs or hex adapters that may be present. Check that the wheels are properly aligned and that any logos or directional tread patterns are pointing in the correct rotation direction.

Tire Replacement: Install the tires on the wheels, making sure the tire bead is securely seated within the wheel rim. To ensure uniform seating, press the tire into the wheel with your fingers or a tire installation tool around the circumference.

Tighten the wheel nuts in the following order: Tighten the wheel nuts or hex nuts to keep the wheels and tires securely in place. Using an appropriate size wrench or socket driver, torque the nuts to the manufacturer's recommendations. Make sure the nuts are evenly tightened to minimize wobbling or unbalance.

Examine the Wheel Alignment: After mounting the wheels, visually inspect them to ensure appropriate alignment. Make any necessary changes to keep the wheels parallel to each other and perpendicular to the chassis for best handling.

Check Clearance for Suspension: Ascertain that the wheels and tires are correctly aligned with the suspension components, chassis, and bodywork. Examine whether the suspension can move freely without being hampered by the wheels or tires.

Tests of rotation and balance: Rotate each wheel by hand to ensure it spins freely and without excessive friction or binding. Inspect the wheels for any wobbling or unbalance, which could indicate improperly mounted tires or damaged wheels. Adjust as necessary to achieve smooth rotation and balance.

Secure Cables and wiring: Make sure any wiring or cables are carefully routed and secured before attaching the wheels and tires. Use zip ties, cable clips, or routing channels to prevent interfering with the wheels, tires, or suspension components.

Conduct a Functionality Test: Test the wheels and tires for functionality before proceeding with further assembly or adjustments. Roll or drive the RC car gently on a flat surface to see how it handles and whether the wheels or tires are damaged. Make any necessary modifications or fine-tuning based on your observations.

Because attachment methods change depending on the model, always follow the instructions in your RC car's manual. Take your time, carefully follow the instructions, and ensure that your RC car's wheels, tires, and axles are properly fitted for optimal performance, stability, and control.

WIRING THE ELECTRONICS (RECEIVER, SERVO, ESC)

Wiring the electronics of your RC car, including the receiver, servo, and electronic speed controller (ESC), is a vital step in ensuring proper control and functionality. Here's a step-by-step guide to assist you with the wiring:

Gather the Required Components: Collect the receiver, servo, ESC, servo extension cables (if needed), and any other wiring and connectors required for your particular RC vehicle model.

Locate the Wiring Ports: Determine the wire ports on the receiver, servo, and ESC of your remote control car. These ports are typically labeled and correspond to certain actions like as throttle, steering, and power.

Connect the Receiver and ESC in the following manner: Begin by connecting the receiver to the ESC. Locate the "Throttle" or "CH1" reception channel and link the

ESC's throttle cable to it. To achieve a secure connection, align the pins and insert the connector firmly.

Attach the Servo: Find the channel labeled "Steering" or "CH2" on the receiver and feed the servo's cable into it. Align the pins once more and insert the connector firmly to ensure a secure connection.

Charge the Recipient: Connect the power wire of the receiver to a suitable power supply. This is usually the ESC's battery port or an auxiliary battery connector. Follow the manufacturer's directions to ensure proper voltage and polarity.

Connect the ESC to the motor as follows: Connect the ESC to the motor wire. Check that the motor wire is firmly soldered or connected to the motor terminals. Consult the manufacturer's instructions for proper wiring setup.

Organize and route the wires: Route the wires neatly around the chassis using zip ties, cable clips, or routing channels. Examine the wire to ensure that it is not pinched or knotted, and that it does not interfere with any moving elements or components.

Connect the battery in the following manner: Connect the positive and negative wires of a separate receiver and servo batteries to the appropriate battery connectors on the receiver or ESC. Pay great attention to the polarity to avoid damaging the electronics.

Perform a Functionality Test: Before turning off the RC car, run a functionality test to ensure that all electronics are operational. Turn on the transmitter and receiver to ensure that the servo responds to steering inputs and that the ESC manages the motor's speed and brakes.

Secure and Tidy the Wiring: Once all electronics are operating, secure and tidy the wiring. To keep the wires organized and out of the way, use adhesive-backed wire clips or zip ties to secure them along the chassis.

Range and operation: Take the RC car for a test drive to confirm the range and performance of the electronics. Check that the transmitter's signals are reaching the receiver in a timely manner and that all controls respond as expected.

Because wire layouts varies depending on the model and manufacturer, always follow the instructions in your RC car's manual. Take your time, carefully follow the instructions, and ensure that all connections are secure and the wire is properly routed for reliable control and operation of your RC car.

CHAPTER SEVEN

FINE-TUNING AND OPTIMIZING THE PERFORMANCE

After you've completed the construction of your RC car, it's time to fine-tune and optimize its performance for the best driving experience. Here are some important steps to help you fine-tune and increase the performance of your RC car:

Suspension and balancing: Check the wheel alignment on your RC car and make any required adjustments. Check that the toe-in and toe-out angles for your model are within the prescribed ranges. Experiment with different suspension settings including ride height, dampening, and spring tension to find the optimum balance for your driving style and terrain.

Modification of the Gear Ratio: Depending on the type of driving you intend to do, you may need to change the gear ratio of your RC car. A higher gear ratio increases top speed, while a lower gear ratio increases acceleration. For instructions on changing the gear ratio, consult your owner's manual, then experiment with several options to find the ideal balance for your needs.

Weight Distribution: Take notice of the weight distribution of your RC car. Check that it is dispersed and balanced evenly between the front and back wheels. By carefully adjusting the batteries or adding weights, you can improve traction and handling.

Fine-tuning To fine-tune the steering and throttle reactions of your RC car, adjust the endpoints and trim settings on your transmitter. This will provide you precise control and response. Experiment with different settings and make modest adjustments until you find the perfect balance for your driving style.

Traction & Tire Selection: Consider the type of terrain you'll be traveling on and choose tires with the most traction. Different tread patterns and rubber compositions work well on various surfaces, including on-road, off-road, and loose dirt. Experiment with different tires to determine which ones provide the most grip and performance for your driving circumstances.

Power and Battery Management: To improve the performance of your RC car's battery, select a suitable battery capacity and chemistry. LiPo batteries, for example, have better power output and longer run times when compared to other battery types.

Additionally, for optimal performance, keep your battery charged and serviced on a regular basis.

Technique Practicing and fine-tuning: Improving your talents as an RC vehicle driver takes time and work. Spend time honing your driving style, experimenting with different corner lines and approaches, and learning how to steer your RC car over various obstacles. You'll get the most out of your RC car if you regularly practice and fine-tune your driving skills.

Seek Professional Assistance: Don't be hesitant to seek assistance from experienced RC vehicle enthusiasts, or to join local RC car groups or internet forums. Participating in the RC car community can provide valuable insights, tips, and tricks for increasing your RC car's performance. Share your knowledge and learn from others who are experienced in tuning and improving RC cars.

Keep in mind that fine-tuning and optimizing the performance of your RC car is an ongoing effort. As you gain experience and get more acquainted with your vehicle's quirks, you'll discover new ways to boost its performance. Enjoy the process of constantly improving and tailoring your RC car to meet your driving preferences and maximize the excitement of the activity.

CHANGING THE SUSPENSION SETTINGS

Adjusting the suspension settings on your RC car is a vital step in optimizing its performance and handling. Here are some important suspension settings to change, along with instructions on how to do so:

Ride Height: Ride height is the distance between the chassis and the ground. By altering the ride height, you can improve the car's stability, cornering ability, and traction. A lower ride height frequently improves stability while sacrificing off-road capabilities, and a higher ride height improves clearance over rough terrain while diminishing stability. You may alter the ride height by adjusting the preload on the suspension springs or using adjustable shock mounts.

The suspension spring tension controls how well the car absorbs bumps and impacts. Firmer springs provide more resistance and are ideally suited for fast tracks or flat land, whilst softer springs allow the vehicle to handle rough terrain and absorb shocks more effectively. Experiment with different spring tensions to find the ideal balance of stability and responsiveness for your driving circumstances.

Damping: The resistance of the shock absorbers determines how quickly the suspension responds to topographic changes. By altering the damping, you may fine-tune the car's capacity to handle bumps and maintain traction. Reduce damping to improve responsiveness and traction on uneven surfaces, or increase damping to improve stability and prevent chassis roll. The damping parameters on most shocks are adjustable via a screw or dial.

When viewed from above, camber is the angle at which the tires lean inward or outward. Negative camber means the tops of the tires are tilting inward, and positive camber means they are tilting outward. When cornering, camber adjustment affects the contact patch of the tires. Positive camber increases straight-line stability while decreasing cornering grip, while negative camber decreases straight-line stability while increasing cornering grip. Experiment with different camber angles to find the ideal setup for your driving style and track conditions.

The toe is the angle at which the tires point inward or outward as viewed from above. Toe-in means the tires are pointing slightly inward, whereas toe-out means the tires are pointing slightly outward. Toe modification affects the vehicle's stability and responsiveness. Toeing in increases stability and straight-line tracking while decreasing turn-in reaction, while toeing out decreases stability while increasing turn-in response. Experiment with different toe placements to find the best balance of stability and cornering performance.

Adjustable anti-roll bars connect the suspension arms on each side of some RC cars. When cornering, anti-roll bars help to control chassis roll and vehicle balance. Increased anti-roll bar stiffness reduces chassis roll and improves stability, whilst decreased rigidity allows for more independent suspension movement and better traction on rough terrain.

When adjusting suspension settings, make one change at a time and watch how it affects the vehicle's performance. Keep track of the modifications you make and the results you get so you can fine-tune the parameters gradually until you achieve the desired performance and handling characteristics. Experimentation and practice are necessary for identifying the ideal suspension configuration for your RC car, so take the time to study how different adjustments effect your car's performance and adapt accordingly.

BALANCING WEIGHT DISTRIBUTION

Your RC car's weight distribution must be optimized for optimal handling, stability, and traction. Here are some ideas for balancing weight distribution:

Consider the current weight distribution: Begin by studying the weight distribution of your RC car. Place the car on a level surface and see whether it leans to the front or back. An imbalance in weight distribution can have an effect on the vehicle's overall performance.

Changing the Battery Position: One of the simplest ways to balance weight distribution is to move the battery. If your RC car has a removable battery, consider moving it closer to the center of the chassis. This change may help with weight distribution between the front and rear wheels. Experiment with alternative battery positions until you achieve a balanced weight distribution.

If changing the battery location does not achieve the desired balance, you can strategically add ballast weights. Ballast weights are small metal plates or weights that can be attached to the chassis or inserted inside the body of an RC car. Place the weights in areas where greater weight is required to achieve the desired balance.

Start with modest weights and gradually increase or decrease as needed.

Suspension Adjustment: Suspension is essential for weight distribution. Adjust the suspension components, such as shock preload and spring tension, to fine-tune the weight distribution. Softer springs at one end can assist in shifting weight to that end, while stiffer springs at the other end can redistribute weight in the other direction. Experiment with different suspension layouts to get the perfect balance.

Consider the following upgrades: To help balance the weight distribution, certain RC car components, like as the motor or electronic speed controller, can be modified. A lighter motor, for example, can shift weight forward, whereas a heavier motor can shift weight backward. Investigate upgrade alternatives for better weight distribution with competent amateurs or manufacturers.

Test and fine-tune: After you've adjusted the weight distribution, take your RC car for a spin. Examine the vehicle's handling, acceleration, and turning. If you see any issues, such as extreme understeer or oversteer, make more tweaks to get the right balance. It may take numerous rounds and changes to find the optimal weight distribution for your RC car and driving style.

Remember that the key to achieving perfect weight distribution is to find the right balance for your specific RC car and driving conditions. Every RC car is unique, and factors such as track surface, driving style, and personal preferences can all influence proper weight distribution. Take your time testing, making little changes and seeing the effects on your car's performance. With patience and dedication, you'll be able to achieve a balanced weight distribution that improves the overall handling and performance of your RC car.

CHAPTER EIGHT

OPTIMIZING GEAR RATIOS

Getting the correct blend of acceleration and top speed requires optimizing your RC car's gear ratios. Here are some recommendations for optimizing gear ratios:

Understand the Basics of Gear Ratios: The gear ratio is calculated by dividing the number of teeth on the pinion gear (attached to the motor) by the number of teeth on the spur gear (attached to the drivetrain). A higher gear ratio (more pinion gear teeth) provides faster acceleration but slower top speed, whereas a lower gear ratio (fewer pinion gear teeth) provides faster acceleration but slower top speed.

Determine Your Driving Needs: Consider the type of driving you'll be undertaking and the characteristics you'd like to improve. If you're usually racing on a broad, open circuit, a higher gear ratio may be acceptable for optimizing top speed. On narrower, trickier tracks or off-road terrain, a lower gear ratio may provide better acceleration and maneuverability.

Look at the present gear ratio: Begin by determining the gear ratio that is currently in use in your RC car. Examine the pinion and spur gear tooth counts. As a starting point for comparison, take note of existing performance metrics such as acceleration and top speed.

Experimentation: Experiment with different pinion and spur gear combinations to optimize the gear ratio. To improve top speed, increase the number of teeth on the pinion gear or decrease the number of teeth on the spur gear. To improve acceleration, reduce the number of teeth on the pinion gear or increase the number of teeth on the spur gear.

Consider the following motor and track factors: The gear ratio you choose should also take into account the power and torque characteristics of your motor. A higher torque motor may necessitate a higher gear ratio in order to fully utilize its power, whereas a lower torque motor may have a lower gear ratio in order to accelerate. Take into account the characteristics of the track or driving surface as well. Long straightaways may call for a higher gear ratio for maximum speed, whilst tight curves may call for a lower gear ratio for faster acceleration out of turns.

Testing and tweaking: Make tiny adjustments to the gear ratio and test your RC car's performance on the track or driving surface. Consider acceleration, top speed, and overall driving comfort. Keep a close eye out for any changes in handling or motor temperature. Adjust the gear ratio slightly until you have the right combination of acceleration and top speed.

Keep an eye on the temperature of the motor: Keep an eye on the temperature of your engine while adjusting gear ratios. If the motor overheats, it could be because the gear ratio is too high, causing the motor to overwork. If this occurs, lessen the strain on the motor and prevent overheating by changing the gear ratio.

Consult with Subject Matter Experts: If you're unsure about which gear ratio to start with or how to optimize it for your specific RC car, seek advice from an experienced hobbyist or the manufacturer. Based on their knowledge and experience with similar arrangements, they can provide advise.

Remember that improving gear ratios is a process of trial and error. Experiment, take notes, and make modest adjustments until you've found the gear ratio that best suits your driving needs and preferences. Enjoy the process of fine-tuning your RC car's performance and determining the best combination of acceleration and top speed for maximum enjoyment on the track or off-road.

CONFIGURATION OF THE TRANSMITTER AND RECEIVER

It is vital to configure your RC car's transmitter and receiver for dependable and responsive control. Here are some pointers to get you started:

Replace the batteries as follows: Begin by replacing the batteries in the transmitter and receiver (also known as the radio controller). To verify that the batteries are correctly inserted and polarized, follow the manufacturer's instructions.

Binding Procedure: To communicate, the transmitter and receiver must be connected. Consult the instruction manuals for your specific transmitter and receiver for more details on the binding method. It is common practice to turn on the transmitter while holding down a specific button or switch, followed by turning on the receiver while holding down a matching button or switch. The LED indicators on both devices will generally provide feedback to signal a successful bind.

Make sure that the transmitter and receiver are on the same channel. Most transmitters have multiple channels to avoid interference with other RC cars. Check that the channel settings on both devices are in sync.

Trims and subtrims: Trims and subtrims let you to fine-tune your RC car's servo neutral position. The neutral position of the transmitter sticks or switches aids in keeping the wheels and controls centered. Using the trim buttons or dials on the transmitter, adjust the trims and subtrims until the servos are suitably positioned.

Endpoint adjustment, also known as servo travel adjustment or ATV (Adjustable Travel Volume), allows you to customize the maximum range of motion of the servos. This setting prevents the servos from moving above their mechanical limits, which might cause strain or binding. Adjust the endpoint parameters using the transmitter's programming options or menu.

Dual Rate Adjustment: You can change the sensitivity or throw of the steering and throttle controls on some transmitters. This feature is extremely useful for fine-tuning the steering response or lowering the top speed of the RC car. Consult your transmitter's handbook for more information on changing dual rates.

Configuration for Fail-Safe: Activate the fail-safe function on your receiver. If the signal between the transmitter and receiver is lost or weakened, the receiver will take a predetermined step to return the RC car to a safe state. This action could be as easy as braking or shifting into neutral. Refer to your receiver's manual for specific instructions on configuring the fail-safe feature.

Range Check: Perform a range check to ensure that both the transmitter and receiver are getting a reliable signal and working within the specified range. Follow the instructions in your transmitter's manual to conduct the range check accurately. This stage assists in identifying any potential signal interference or weak signal spots.

Calibration and testing: After connecting the transmitter and receiver, do a thorough testing and calibration session. Check that all controls respond correctly and smoothly, and that the steering, throttle, and other functions function properly. Drive the RC car in various directions and distances to evaluate the control's range and response.

Remember to read the manuals for your transmitter and receiver for complete instructions as well as any additional features unique to your equipment. Setting up the transmitter and receiver correctly results in a dependable and enjoyable RC car driving experience.

RESOLVING COMMON BUILD ISSUES

You may encounter some common hurdles that can hinder your progress while making an RC car. Here are some troubleshooting tips to help you with these build issues:

Loose or misaligned components: Inspect the affected area carefully if you find any loose or misaligned components, such as screws, nuts, or suspension elements. Tighten any loose screws or fasteners with the appropriate tools. Check that all components are aligned appropriately according to the assembly instructions or schematics.

Inadequate electrical connections: Electrical connections that are inconsistent or unstable may cause performance issues with the vehicle. Check all electrical connections, including battery connectors, motor cables, and servo connections. Ascertain that they are safe and in proper contact. As needed, clean the connectors and terminals to remove any dirt or corrosion.

If you're encountering issues with the motor or the electronic speed controller (ESC), check the wire connections first. Check that the motor wires are properly soldered and securely connected to the ESC. If the motor isn't working, ensure sure the ESC is getting power and that the throttle signals from the transmitter are being received appropriately. Consult the manufacturer's instructions for addressing individual motor or ESC difficulties.

Steering Problems: If you're having steering issues, such as unresponsive or erratic behavior, double-check the servo connections and make sure they're securely inserted into the receiver. Check that the servo horn is aligned with the steering linkage and that the servo is centered. Use the trim and subtrim settings on the transmitter to fine-tune the servo's neutral position.

Suspension Concerns: Check the suspension components, such as shocks, A-arms, or suspension arms, if your suspension isn't working properly. Examine for any signs of binding, excessive friction, or damage. Ascertain that the suspension components move freely and smoothly. Lubricate the suspension pivots as needed. Adjust the shock preload and damping settings to achieve the desired suspension performance.

If you are having signal interference or range problems,

ensure sure your transmitter's antenna is fully stretched and undamaged. Keep the transmitter antenna away from any metal objects or sources of interference. Perform a range check to identify any areas with poor signal. Use a different frequency or channel if possible, or switch to a 2.4GHz wireless system that is less prone to interference.

Excessive heat from the motor, electronic components, or batteries may indicate a problem. Check the airflow around these components to verify it is not obstructed or coated. Excessive heat may indicate an overloaded or incorrectly configured system. Check that the gear ratio, motor timing, and ESC settings are accurate for your system.

Inadequate Battery Performance: If your batteries deplete quickly or provide inconsistent power, check their voltage levels and overall health. Make certain that you are using appropriate and completely charged batteries. If battery performance is an issue, consider upgrading to larger-capacity or higher-quality batteries.

Consult the manufacturer's resources: If you encounter reoccurring problems or problems that are unique to your RC car kit or components, consult the manufacturer's resources. Look for troubleshooting guides, FAQs, or customer forums where you can seek guidance from experienced users or the manufacturer's technical support team.

Remember to troubleshoot in a systematic fashion, addressing one issue at a time and referring to appropriate documentation and resources. Patience and thorough debugging will assist you in identifying and resolving typical construction challenges, delivering an enjoyable and successful RC car building experience.

PAINTING AND CUSTOMIZING YOUR RC CAR

Painting and personalizing your RC car is a great way to put a personal touch to it and set it apart from the crowd. Here are some pointers to help you get a professional-looking paint job and customize your RC car:

Preparation:

Clean the RC car well to remove any dirt, grease, or dust. Clean it with a mild detergent and water, then thoroughly dry it.

Disassemble any removable pieces, such as the body shell, wing, or bumpers, to make painting easier.

To create a smooth and slightly roughened surface for improved paint application, use fine-grit sandpaper.

Priming: Use a primer designed specifically for RC vehicle bodies. Priming enhances paint adhesion and provides a smooth surface for color applications.

Follow the manufacturer's instructions when applying the primer. It is frequently sprayed on in thin coats, with each coat drying before applying the next.

Paint Choice:

Select a high-quality RC car body paint that is appropriate for the body material you have (for example, polycarbonate or lexan).

Spray paints made specifically for RC car bodies offer exceptional coverage, flexibility, and durability.

Choose your design's hue or colors and gather all of the necessary paints and materials, such as masking tape or stencils.

Making Use of the Base Color:

Begin by applying the basic color to the body shell. Maintain a distance of 6-8 inches (15-20 cm) between the spray can and the surface.

Paint in thin, even coats, using smooth, sweeping motions with the can. Avoid spraying too close or staying in one spot for too long to avoid drips or uneven coverage.

Allow each layer to cure before applying extra coats, as directed by the manufacturer.

Personalization and detailing:

Using masking tape or stencils, create your own drawings, patterns, or graphics on the body shell. Tape or stencil the places you don't want to get paint on.

Using the same thin, even coatings approach, spray the desired custom colors or additional layers over the masked regions.

Experiment with several techniques to achieve the desired look, such as fading, blending, or adding details with brushes or airbrushing.

Apply a clear protective coat over the whole body shell once the paint has completely hardened. The clear coat enhances the brilliance, longevity, and protection of the paint finish.

Apply the clear coat as directed by the manufacturer, ensuring even coverage and allowing ample drying time between layers.

Remove any masking tape or stencils from the body shell when the paint has completely dried.

Reassemble the RC car, making sure to secure the painted body shell and any other special components.

Additional Personalization: To improve the overall aesthetic of your RC car, consider adding decals, stickers, or sponsor logos.

Consider customizing other components, such as wheels, tires, or spoilers, to compliment your personalized body shell.

Use a paint booth or work in a well-ventilated location to guarantee optimum airflow and safety. Take your time, be patient, and practice on scrap materials or spare pieces before attempting more complicated patterns. With careful planning and attention to detail, you can create a stunning and one-of-a-kind paint work that shows your own style and imagination.

MAINTAINING AND UPGRADING YOUR RC CAR

Maintaining and upgrading your RC car is crucial for best performance and lifetime. Here are some important tips to help you keep your RC car in good condition and examine upgrading options:

Cleaning: Clean your RC car after each usage to remove dirt, dust, and debris. Use a soft brush or compressed air to clean hard-to-reach areas.

Remove the body shell to clean the chassis, suspension components, and drivetrain thoroughly.

Before reinstalling, clean the body shell with a mild detergent and water, then thoroughly dry it.

Routine inspections should be performed to search for signs of wear, damage, or loose parts.

Examine the tires for wear and tear, and replace them if necessary.

Look for signs of wear or excessive play in the suspension

components. Tighten any loose screws or bolts.

Examine the gears, drivetrain, and motor for unusual noises, wear, or misalignment. Address any flaws as quickly as possible to minimize further damage.

Lubrication: As needed, lubricate moving parts such as bearings, gears, and suspension pivot points.

Use silicone-based lubricants for plastic components and specialised lubricants for metal parts.

Apply lubricants with care and wipe away any excess to avoid collection and dirt attraction.

Battery Care: Charge and store your RC car batteries as directed by the manufacturer.

Use a decent balancing charger to charge your batteries and prevent overcharging or discharging them excessively.

Keep your batteries cool and dry, away from direct sunlight and extreme heat.

Upgrades: Investigate upgrade options for your RC car; upgrades can increase overall performance, longevity, and enjoyment.

Consider changing components such as the motor, ESC, suspension, shocks, or transmission to improve speed, handling, or lifetime.

Consider your specific needs and objectives for the RC car, and then choose improvements that match to your desired performance gains.

Modifications and tuning:

Experiment with different tuning options to boost the performance of your RC car.

Adjust suspension characteristics such as ride height, shock firmness, and camber to fine-tune handling and traction.

Examine different gear ratios to achieve the desired balance of acceleration and top speed.

Make minor adjustments and track performance changes to find the ideal setup for your driving style and track conditions.

Suggestions for the Track and the Environment:

Take into account the track or environment in which you will be driving your RC car.

Select tires and tread patterns appropriate for the surface you'll be going on, such as on-road or off-road tires.

Suspension and ride height should be modified in accordance with the terrain or track conditions.

Weather conditions should be taken into account, since extreme temperatures or dampness can have an effect on the performance and durability of your RC car.

Seek Expert Advice: Join RC vehicle groups, forums, or local clubs to connect with seasoned hobbyists.

Attend RC car races or events to learn about maintenance and upgrade processes from experienced racers.

Consult the manufacturer's resources, such as online forums, manuals, or support channels, for specific maintenance and upgrade needs.

Regular maintenance and modifications will not only extend the life of your RC car, but will also improve its performance and enjoyment factor. By committing time to maintenance and exploring upgrade options, you may continue to push the limits of your RC car and enjoy many hours of thrilling driving experiences.

TROUBLESHOOTING AND REGULAR PROBLEMS

While RC cars can provide hours of exciting amusement, they are not without technological issues and challenges. Here are some general troubleshooting approaches to help you resolve common issues and get your remote control car back on track:

The remote control car does not turn on or respond.

Check that the battery or power supply is properly connected and charged. Replace or recharge the battery as needed. Examine the electrical connections for any loose or damaged wires. If you're using a remote control, make sure the batteries are fully charged.

Slow acceleration or poor performance is a problem.

Solution: Examine the drivetrain and transmission for debris, grime, or worn-out parts. Clean or replace components as needed. Check that the motor is operational and not overheated. Change the gear ratio to boost acceleration and speed.

Inspect the tires for proper inflation and traction.

The RC car does not steer and makes unexpected turns.

Examine the steering system for any loose or worn-out components. Tighten or replace components as needed. Check the servo and its connection to ensure it is working properly. Adjust the steering trim with your remote control to fine-tune the steering response.

The issue: insufficient battery life or a limited runtime.

Solution: Check the battery capacity to check that it is sufficient for your RC car. Consider upgrading to a larger-capacity battery if necessary. To save electricity, avoid using the throttle too much and driving aggressively. Charge and store your batteries as directed by the manufacturer.

Excessive heat generated by a motor or an electrical component.

Solution: Ensure proper airflow and cooling for the motor and electronic components. Look for any obstacles or debris in the ventilation system. Adjust gear ratios or throttle usage to reduce motor strain. Consider upgrading to a more efficient motor or electronic components that can dissipate heat better.

Parts that are loose or removed are a source of concern.

Solution: On a regular basis, inspect and tighten all screws, bolts, and nuts on your RC car. Use thread-locking chemicals if necessary to keep them from loosening during operation. Any broken or missing parts should be replaced as soon as feasible.

The remote control is not responding or is acting strangely.

Check and replace the batteries in your remote control as needed. Make sure the remote control and receiver are properly paired and within range of one another. Check the radio for any interference or signal obstructions. If the issues persist, think about upgrading to a higher-quality remote control system.

Unusual noises or vibrations are a source of concern.

Solution: To establish the cause of the noise or vibration, examine many components such as gears, drivetrain, suspension, and wheel axles. Check the object for evidence of damage or wear. Tighten any loose connections and grease any moving parts. Any worn-out or broken components should be replaced.

If you encounter more sophisticated or persistent issues with your RC car, consult the manufacturer's documentation, internet forums, or seek assistance from experienced RC car enthusiasts. Don't be afraid to ask for help; the RC community is always happy to share their knowledge and offer guidance. To correctly uncover and resolve the issue, remember to approach troubleshooting with patience and a thorough approach.

COMPREHENDING ELECTRONIC PROBLEMS AND TROUBLESHOOTING TECHNIQUES

Electronic difficulties in RC cars might occur on occasion, jeopardizing their performance and functionality. Here are some common electronic difficulties and troubleshooting solutions for dealing with them:

Unresponsive or unpredictable controls are a concern.

Troubleshooting: Check that the transmitter and receiver are properly connected. Check to see if they are properly paired and in range. Check that both the transmitter and receiver batteries are charged and, if necessary, replaced. Adjust the trim settings on the transmitter to fine-tune the control response. Examine the vicinity for any electrical equipment or radio waves that may be causing interference.

Power outages or shutdowns are a recurring issue.

Troubleshooting: Make sure the battery connections are snug.

Check the battery voltage to make sure it is within the allowed range. Replace the battery if it is worn out or no longer holds a charge. Examine the wiring for any loose or broken connections. Look for defects or problems with the power switch and its wiring.

Problems with the ESC (Electronic Speed Controller).

Troubleshooting: Check that the programming settings on the ESC are correct for your RC car and motor. Restore the ESC to factory settings and reprogram if necessary. Look for any loose or broken connections in the motor wiring. Check that the ESC's cooling system is operational, as overheating might cause problems. Update the ESC firmware if the manufacturer supplies it.

The motor or servo is broken.

Troubleshooting: Verify that the motor or servo connections are correctly attached. Look for any loose or damaged connections in the cables and connectors. Connect the motor or servo directly to a power source to see if it is working properly. Replace the motor or servo if it is broken or damaged.

There is a problem with receiver interference or signal loss.

Troubleshooting: Look for any physical obstructions that could interfere with the signal between the transmitter and the receiver. Keep a safe distance between the receiving antenna and any metal components or wiring that may cause interference. Consider increasing the signal receiving capability of your receiver or installing a signal amplifier. Choose a frequency or channel with the least amount of interference if you're using a multi-channel transmitter.

Excessive heat is a concern with electrical components.

Troubleshooting: Check that all electronic components, including as the ESC, motor, and receiver, are adequately ventilated and cooled. Examine the airflow for any impediments and clear away any accumulated debris. Changing gear ratios or using the throttle lessens the strain on electronic components. Install additional cooling mechanisms, such as heatsinks or fans, to dissipate heat more effectively.

Problems with programming or configuration.

Troubleshooting: Refer to the user manual or manufacturer's documentation for information on programming or configuring electronic components. Check that the programming sequence or steps are followed correctly. Restore the electronic components to their factory settings and, if necessary, reprogram. Contact the manufacturer's support or search online forums for help with specific programming issues.

When troubleshooting electronic problems, remember to proceed with caution and to follow the manufacturer's safety guidelines. If you are unsure or uncomfortable handling electronic components, get assistance from experienced people or professional RC car experts. Manufacturer documentation, online forums, and community sites can also be valuable for troubleshooting your RC car model and electronic components.

RESOLVING MECHANICAL PROBLEMS

Mechanical issues are common when dealing with RC cars. Here are some common mechanical issues and troubleshooting procedures to assist you in resolving them:

The problem is a grinding or clicking sound coming from the drivetrain.

Troubleshooting: Examine the drivetrain gears for signs of wear, breakage, or misalignment. Any worn or broken gears should be replaced. Check that the gears are properly lubricated. To ensure smooth operation, check the tightness of the gear mesh between the gears. Fine-tune the gear mesh as needed.

Problem: Slippery tires or poor traction.

Examine the tires for wear and replace them as needed. Remove any debris or foreign substances that may be interfering with traction by cleaning the tires. Adjust tire pressure to improve grip. Consider using different tires or tire compounds suitable for the surface you are driving on. Examine the differential for flaws and make any required modifications.

Suspension bottoming out or inadequate damping is the issue.

Troubleshooting: Adjust the ride height and preload of the suspension to prevent it from bottoming out. Examine the suspension springs for wear or damage and, if necessary, repair them. Adjust the damping settings on the shocks to get the greatest suspension performance. Upgrade to adjustable or higher-quality shocks for improved suspension control.

The problem is unstable or loose wheels.

Troubleshooting: Make sure the wheel hexes or axle hubs are securely secured. Tighten any wheel nuts or screws that are loose. Examine the wheel bearings for wear or damage and replace them as necessary. Make that the wheels are properly balanced and aligned. To guarantee proper wheel alignment, adjust the camber and toe settings.

Excessive vibration or shaking is the problem.

Troubleshooting: Check the wheel and tire balance. Wheel weights or a balancer can be used to balance them. Inspect the drivetrain components for signs of damage or misalignment, such as driveshafts and axles. Any worn or broken components should be realigned or replaced. To eliminate vibrations, make sure all screws and nuts are securely fastened.

The steering is either stiff or sluggish.

Troubleshooting: Look for binding or obstructions in the steering components, such as the servo and linkage. Lubricate the steering system's moving parts. Examine the servo for proper operation and, if necessary, adjust its settings. Make that the servo horn is correctly aligned with the steering assembly. To fine-tune the steering response, adjust the steering trim on the transmitter.

Excessive motor heat or overheating is a problem.

Troubleshooting: Make sure the motor gearing is suitable for the application. Reduce the load on the motor by adjusting the gear ratio as needed. Make that the motor is properly cooled and that the cooling vents are not blocked. Examine the motor for debris or grime and clean it as needed. Consider adding additional cooling mechanisms, such as heatsinks or fans, to more effectively remove heat.

Suspension components that are loose or damaged are the source of the problem.

Troubleshooting: Look for signs of wear, damage, or looseness in the suspension arms, shock towers, and other suspension components. Tighten any unsecured screws or bolts. Any broken or damaged parts should be replaced. Make sure the suspension is properly lubricated for smooth functioning.

Adjust suspension settings such as ride height and shock firmness to optimize performance.

Keep in mind that troubleshooting mechanical errors may require some trial and error. It is vital to approach the assignment patiently and methodically. If you are unsure about the problem or how to solve it, consult the manufacturer's documentation, seek advice from experienced RC enthusiasts, or consider taking your RC car to a professional for help.

THE END

Made in the USA
Columbia, SC
25 February 2024

32254302R00130